FIRST EXPERIENCES

NASIR'S NEW SISTER

by Mari Schuh
illustrated by Daniela Massironi

GRASSHOPPER

Tools for Parents & Teachers

Grasshopper Books enhance imagination and introduce the earliest readers to fiction with fun storylines and illustrations. The easy-to-read text supports early reading experiences with repetitive sentence patterns and sight words.

Before Reading

- Look at the cover illustration. What do readers see? What do they think the book will be about?
- Look at the picture glossary together. Sound out the words. Ask readers to identify the first letter of each vocabulary word.

Read the Book

- "Walk" through the book, reading to or along with the reader. Point to the illustrations as you read.

After Reading

- Review the picture glossary again. Ask readers to locate the words in the text.
- Ask the reader: How did Nasir feel when his baby sister came home? How did he feel later? How do you know?

Grasshopper Books are published by Jump!
5357 Penn Avenue South
Minneapolis, MN 55419
www.jumplibrary.com

Library of Congress Cataloging-in-Publication Data

Names: Schuh, Mari C., 1975- author.
Massironi, Daniela, illustrator.
Title: Nasir's new sister / by Mari Schuh;
illustrated by Daniela Massironi.
Description: Minneapolis, MN: Jump!, Inc., [2023]
Series: First experiences
Audience: Ages 4-7.
Identifiers: LCCN 2021059759 (print)
LCCN 2021059760 (ebook)
ISBN 9781636909301 (hardcover)
ISBN 9781636909318 (paperback)
ISBN 9781636909325 (ebook)
Subjects: LCSH: Readers (Primary)
Brothers and sisters–Juvenile fiction.
LCGFT: Readers (Publications)
Classification: LCC PE1119.2 .S376 2023 (print)
LCC PE1119.2 (ebook)
DDC 428.6/2–dc23/eng/20211215
LC record available at https://lccn.loc.gov/2021059759
LC ebook record available at https://lccn.loc.gov/2021059760

Editor: Jenna Gleisner
Direction and Layout: Anna Peterson
Illustrator: Daniela Massironi

Printed in the United States of America at
Corporate Graphics in North Mankato, Minnesota.

Table of Contents

A New Sister

"Nasir, meet your new baby sister!" Mom says. "This is Salma."

"I made you this," I say.

But Salma doesn't smile.

"She doesn't like it," I say.

"She is too young to understand," Dad says. "That was very nice of you, Nasir. We will put it in her room."

Mom puts Salma in her crib.

Salma cries.

"Can she be quiet?
She is so loud!" I yell.

"Shh! It is OK," Mom says.
"She is just tired."

I want to play.

But Dad is busy.

"You never play with me anymore!" I say.

"Do you want to help?" Dad asks.

I help dress Salma.

She smiles at me!

"Nice job, Nasir! Thank you for helping," Dad says.

Then I help feed her.

“You are a good big brother,”
Mom says.

“I love you, Salma,” I say
to my new baby sister.

Let's Review!

In what ways does Nasir help his baby sister?

A. He plays catch with her.
B. He helps dress her.
C. He reads her a story.
D. He helps feed her.

Picture Glossary

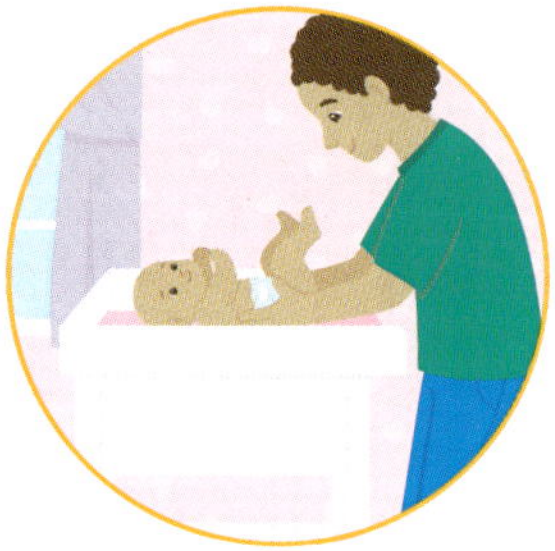

busy
Having a lot to do.

crib
A small bed for a baby with bars on the sides.

dress
To put clothes on.

feed
To give food to.

Let's Review! Answer Key: **B.** He helps dress her. **D.** He helps feed her.